The Story of Noah
La Historia de Noé

The Story of Noah
La Historia de Noé

by Patricia A. Pingry

Illustrated by
Stacy Venturi-Pickett

ideals children's books.
Nashville, Tennessee

ISBN-13: 978-0-8249-4135-2

ISBN-10: 0-8249-4135-7

Published by Ideals Children's Books

An imprint of Ideals Publications, a Guideposts Company

Nashville, Tennessee

www.idealsbooks.com

Printed and bound in Mexico by RR Donnelley

Library of Congress Cataloging-in-Publication Data

Pingry, Patricia.

The story of Noah = La historia de Noé / by Patricia A. Pingry ; illustrated by Stacy Venturi-Pickett.

p. cm.

Summary: A simple retelling of the Biblical story from Genesis in which Noah builds an ark to save his family and two of each animal from a flood that covers the earth.

ISBN-10: 0-8249-4135-7 (alk. paper)

1. Noah (Biblical figure)--Juvenile literature. 2. Noah's ark--Juvenile literature. 3. Deluge--Juvenile literature. [1. Noah (Biblical figure) 2. Noah's ark. 3. Bible stories--O.T. 4. Spanish language materials--Bilingual.] I. Title: Historia de Noé. II. Venturi-Pickett, Stacy, 1963- III. Title.

BS580.N6 P56 2001

222'.1109505--dc21   2001035817

To Parents and Teachers:

The Story of Noah, La Historia de Noé, is one of a series of bilingual books specially created by Ideals Children's Books to help children and their parents learn to read both Spanish and English through a familiar Bible story.

If the child's first language is English, he or she will understand and be able to read the text on the left-hand pages of this book. If the child wishes to read Spanish, he or she will be able to read the right-hand pages of the book. Whether the child's native language is English or Spanish, he or she will be able to compare the text of the two pages and, thus, learn to read both English and Spanish.

Also included at the end of the story are several common words listed in both English and Spanish that the child may review. These include both nouns, with their gender in Spanish, and verbs. In the case of the verbs, the Spanish verbs have the endings that indicate their use in the story.

Parents and teachers will want to use this book as a beginning reader for children who speak either English or Spanish.

A los Padres y los Maestros:

The Story of Noah, La Historia de Noé es parte de una serie de libros bilingüe hecho especialmente por Ideals Children's Books para ayudar a los niños y a sus padres a aprender como leer en los dos idiomas, español e inglés, por medio de un cuento familiar de la Biblia.

Si el primer idioma del niño es inglés, él puede leer y entender lo que está escrito en la página a la izquierda. Si el niño quiere leer en español, él puede leer las páginas a la derecha. Cualquiera que sea el idioma nativo, el inglés o el español, el niño podrá comparar lo escrito en las dos páginas y entonces aprenderá como leer en inglés y en español.

Al final de la historia es incluida para repasar una lista de varias palabras comunes en el inglés y el español. La lista tiene ambos nombres, con el género y verbos en español con los fines que indican el uso en la historia.

Los padres y los maestros tendrán ganas de usar este librito como libro principio para niños que hablan inglés o español.

A long time ago God said to Noah,
"You must build a big boat."

Hace mucho tiempo Dios le dijo a Noé:

"Construye un gran barco."

So Noah built a big boat just as God said.
The boat was called the ark.

Así que Noé construyó un gran barco, exactamente como Dios le dijo. El barco se llamó el arca.

Noah's friends laughed at him. "That Noah is crazy," they said. "It never rains in this desert."

Los amigos de Noé se rieron de él. "Ese Noé está loco," dijeron. "Nunca llueve en este desierto."

One day,
two leopards
came to
the ark.
Then two
elephants
came.

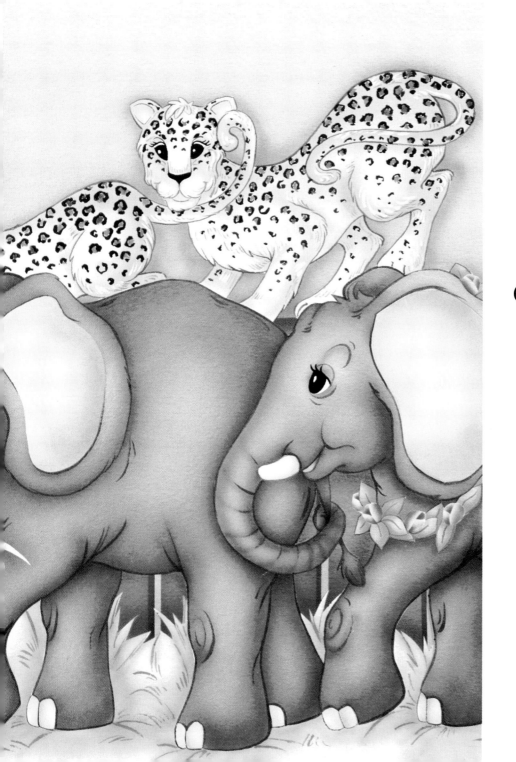

Un día,
entraron dos
leopardos
al arca.
Luego, dos
elefantes.

God sent two of every animal
on earth to Noah's ark.

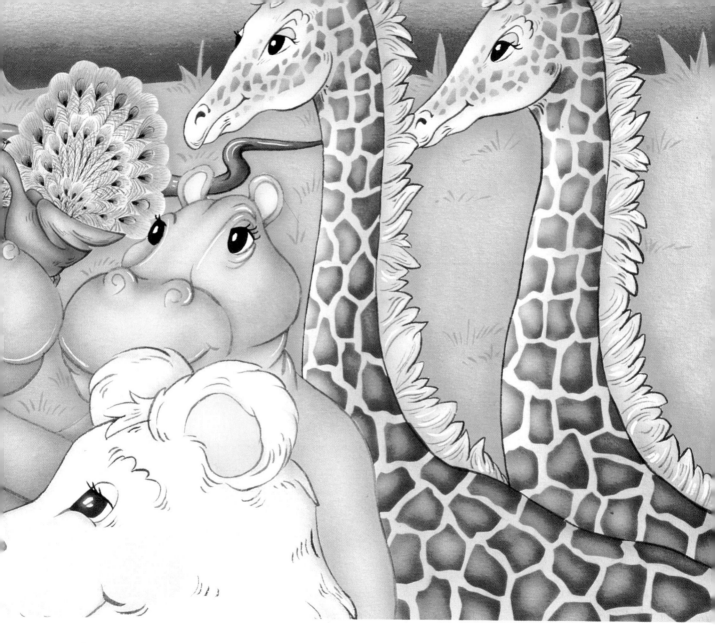

Dios envió una pareja de cada animal
de la tierra al arca de Noé.

After the animals were inside the ark,
Noah went in too. God shut the door.

Después de que los animales estuvieron dentro del arca, Noé entró también. Dios cerró la puerta.

Plop! went the raindrops. Crash! went the lightning
Boom! went the thunder. Noah was not afraid.

¡Plaf! se escucharon las gotas de lluvia.

¡Crash! se vio un relámpago. ¡Pum!

se escucharon los truenos. Noé no se asustó.

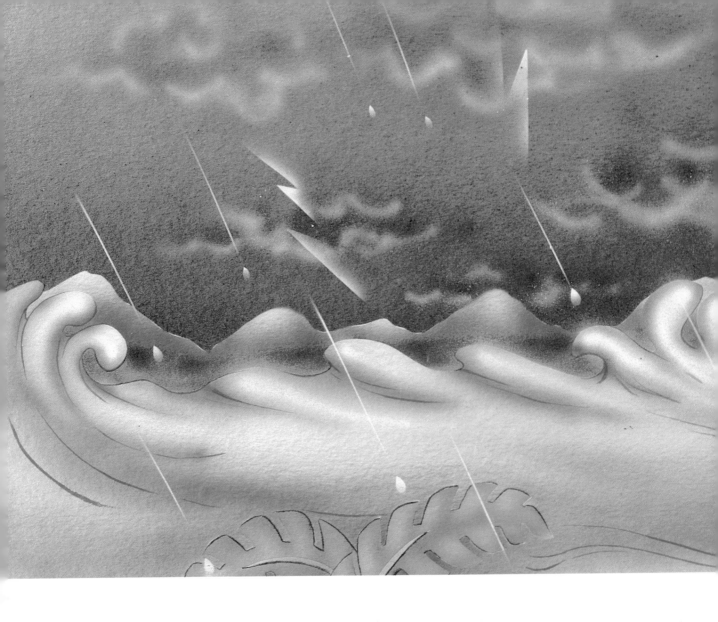

The water rose higher and higher.

The ark began to float.

El agua creció más y más alto.

El arca comenzó a flotar.

It rained forty days and forty nights.
Then the rain stopped. The water went down.

Llovió cuarenta días y cuarenta noches.
Después, dejó de llover. El agua comenzó a bajar.

The land was dry. Noah and the animals prayed, "Thank you, God, for a beautiful, clean world."

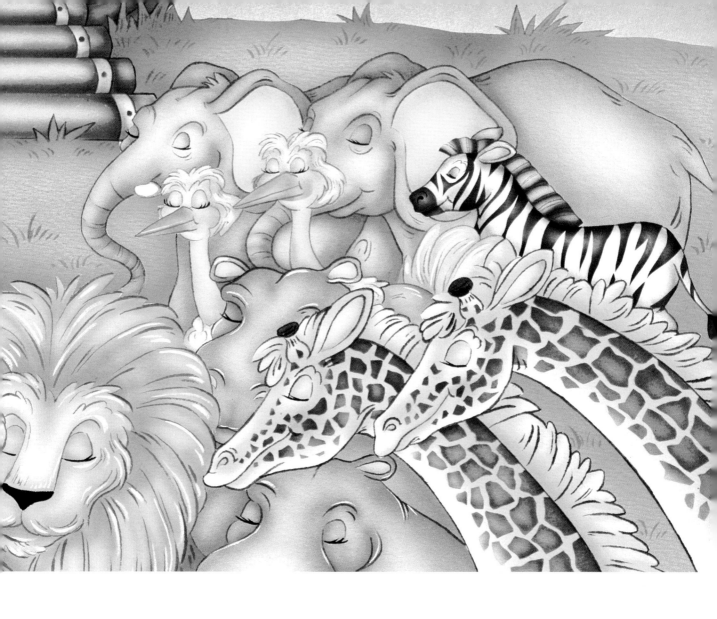

La tierra se secó. Noé y los animales rezaron diciendo:

"Gracias, Dios, por darnos un mundo maravilloso y limpio."

Noah looked up and saw colored stripes
in the sky. This was the very first rainbow.

Noé volteó hacia arriba y vio rayas de colores en el cielo. Este fue el primer arco iris.

"Look for My rainbow
after every rain,"
God said. "It means
I love you."

"Busquen Mi arco iris después de cada lluvia," dijo Dios. "Significa que los amo."

Vocabulary words used in

The Story of Noah
La Historia de Noé

English	Spanish	English	Spanish
story	la historia	crazy	loco
Noah	Noé	never	nunca
God	Dios	rains	llueve
time	el tiempo	this	este
he said	dijo	desert	el desierto
big	gran	day	el día
boat	el barco	two	dos
so	así que	leopards	los leopardos
he built	construyó	they came	entraron
just	exactamente	then	luego
as	como	elephants	los elefantes
it was called	se llamó	he sent	envió
ark	el arca	pair	una pareja
friends	los amigos	every	cada
they laughed	se rieron	animal	el animal
him	él	earth	la tierra
that	ese	after	después

English	Spanish	English	Spanish
inside	dentro de	night	la noche
he entered	entró	it stopped	dejó
too	también	to go down	bajar
he shut	cerró	they prayed	rezaron
door	la puerta	thank you	gracias
raindrops	las gotas de lluvia	clean	limpio
lightning	el relámpago	up	arriba
thunder	los truenos	he saw	vio
was not afraid	no se asustó	stripes	las rayas
water	la agua	colors (n)	los colores
it rose	creció	sky	el cielo
higher	alto	first	primer
and	y	rainbow	el arco iris
it began	comenzó	they look for	busquen
to float	flotar	my	mi
it rained	llovió	it means	significa
forty	cuarenta	I love	amo